Gold and Silver Mining Stocks Guide For Beginners

Roggie Clark

Learn How To Invest in Gold Bars With This Book

Whether you're new to investing or seeking to diversify your portfolio, this beginner-friendly guide will give you the knowledge and confidence to invest in gold, and other precious metals.

https://www.amazon.com/Ultimate-Investing-Buying-Guide-Beginners-ebook/dp/B0F1KWWDXG

Learn How To Invest in Physical Silver With This Book

Whether you're approaching retirement or already enjoying it, protecting and growing your wealth is critical. The Ultimate Silver Investing & Buying Guide For Beginners is your clear, no-nonsense guide to incorporating silver into your wealth-building strategy.

https://www.amazon.com/Ultimate-Silver-Investing-Buying-Beginners-ebook

Learn Macro and Micro Economics, With This One Book

Whether you're a student, a professional, or simply someone eager to understand the world around you, this book is your perfect introduction to the fundamentals of micro and macroeconomics.

https://www.amazon.com/Macro-Micro-Economics-Made-Beginners-ebook/dp/B0DPHTFVQG

Copyright

Title: Gold and Silver Mining Stocks For Beginners
Author: Roggie Clark

Cover Design: Roggie Clark
Editing: Renee' Clark

Printed in the United States of America

Disclaimer

The views and opinions expressed in this book are those of the author and do not necessarily reflect the official policy or position of any individual, company, or organization cited or referenced in the text.

The author is not affiliated with any of the individuals, companies, or organizations mentioned in the text, nor does the author receive any form of compensation for citing or referencing them. Some sample scenarios in this text are fictitious. Any similarity to actual persons, living or dead, is purely coincidental.

The professional information (strategies, tips, and concepts) in this text is provided on an "as is" basis, without warranties of any kind, express or implied. While every effort has been made to ensure the accuracy of the information contained herein, neither the author nor the publisher makes any representations or warranties regarding its completeness, reliability, or applicability. The information is for educational and informational purposes only and should not be interpreted as professional, legal, financial, or business advice.

This book does **not** constitute financial advice, investment guidance, or legal counsel. Any financial, business, or investment decisions made based on this book are done **at your own risk**. You should always conduct your own research and consult a **certified financial**

advisor, legal professional, or other qualified expert before making any decisions that could impact your finances, business, or legal standing.

Neither the author nor the publisher guarantees any specific results or outcomes. By reading this book, you acknowledge and agree that the author and publisher shall not be held liable for any direct, indirect, incidental, or consequential damages, financial losses, or harm arising from the use or misuse of the information contained in this text. You assume full responsibility for any actions taken based on the content of this book.

Table of Contents

Introduction

If you have been paying attention to financial markets over the past few years, you have likely noticed that gold and silver tend to attract attention during periods of economic uncertainty. Inflation, interest rate changes, geopolitical tension, and concerns about currency stability often push investors to explore precious metals as a way to preserve purchasing power.

While many investors choose to own physical gold or silver, others are drawn to mining stocks. The appeal is understandable. Mining companies offer exposure to precious metals through publicly traded shares, which means they can be bought and sold just like any other stock. In theory, when gold or silver prices rise, mining companies may become more profitable. This possibility creates the narrative that mining stocks provide "leveraged exposure" to metals.

However, owning shares in a mining company is very different from owning physical gold or silver. When you buy a mining stock, you are investing in a business. That business has management teams, operational costs, geopolitical exposure, debt obligations, regulatory challenges, and shareholder pressures. Its performance is influenced not only by metal prices, but also by corporate decisions, production efficiency, and broader equity market conditions.

Because of this, gold and silver mining stocks deserve careful examination. This book is not designed to sell you on mining stocks, nor is it designed to discourage you from them. The goal is education before speculation. Before allocating capital, it is important to understand how these companies operate, what risks they carry, and why their stock prices do not always move in lockstep with gold or silver.

Throughout this book, we will explore how mining companies generate revenue, how costs impact profitability, and how different types of mining firms carry different levels of risk. We will examine operational and financial challenges that beginners often overlook. We will also discuss behavioral economic patterns that influence investor decision making, especially during bull markets when excitement can overshadow analysis.

By the end of this book, you should have a clearer understanding of what gold and silver mining stocks truly represent. Whether you ultimately decide to invest or decide they do not fit your strategy, the decision should be based on knowledge rather than narrative.

In the next chapter, we will begin with the fundamentals by answering a simple but important question: what exactly are gold and silver mining stocks?

Chapter 1: What Are Gold and Silver Mining Stocks?

When people hear the term gold or silver investing, they often think about coins, bullion, or bars. Mining stocks are different. Instead of owning physical metal, you are purchasing shares of a company that explores for, develops, and produces gold or silver. That distinction may sound simple, but it changes everything about the investment.

Before we talk about risks, leverage, or speculation, we need to understand what these companies actually are and what you are truly buying when you purchase their stock.

Understanding Publicly Traded Mining Companies

Gold and silver mining companies are businesses listed on public stock exchanges. Investors can buy shares in these companies just like they would buy shares of a technology firm, a bank, or a retail company.

These companies are responsible for:

- Exploring land to locate gold or silver deposits
- Securing permits and regulatory approvals
- Building and operating mining facilities

- Extracting and processing ore
- Selling refined metal into the market

Their revenue depends on their ability to efficiently extract metals and sell them at prices that exceed their operational costs. In other words, they are industrial businesses first. The metal price matters, but execution matters just as much.

When you buy a mining stock, you are not buying gold or silver directly. You are buying partial ownership in a corporation.

Mining Stocks vs Owning Physical Metal

This is an important distinction.

Owning physical gold or silver means you hold a tangible asset. Its value is tied directly to the spot price of the metal, minus premiums and transaction costs.

Owning a mining stock means you own equity in a company. That company has:

- Management teams
- Employees

- Debt obligations
- Operational risks
- Shareholders
- Regulatory exposure

Even if gold prices rise, a mining company can still struggle if it mismanages costs, overextends itself financially, or faces production setbacks.

Physical metal has price risk. Mining stocks have both price risk and business risk.

Why Investors Are Drawn to Mining Stocks

Mining stocks attract attention for several reasons.

First, they offer accessibility. Buying shares through a brokerage account is often easier than arranging secure storage for physical metals.

Second, mining companies can sometimes outperform gold or silver prices during strong bull markets. If a company's production costs remain stable while metal prices rise, profit margins can expand. That potential expansion creates the perception of amplified returns.

Third, mining stocks are part of the broader equity market. This means they can be included in retirement accounts, traded actively, or integrated into diversified portfolios alongside other stocks.

For some investors, that flexibility is appealing.

The Leverage Narrative Explained

You may often hear that mining stocks provide leverage to gold or silver prices. This idea is based on operating margins.

Here is the simplified concept:

- If gold is selling for $2,000 per ounce
- And a mining company's cost to produce it is $1,500 per ounce
- The company earns $500 per ounce in margin

If gold rises to $2,200 and costs remain stable:

- The margin increases to $700 per ounce

That is a 40 percent increase in profit margin from a 10 percent move in gold.

This is why mining stocks can move more aggressively than the metals themselves. However, leverage works both ways. If gold prices fall, margins compress just as quickly.

Understanding this dynamic is important because it highlights the amplified nature of mining equities compared to physical metal.

Common Beginner Misconceptions

Beginners often assume that mining stocks and gold prices move in perfect synchronization. In reality, that is not always the case.

Some common misunderstandings include:

- Assuming every mining company is profitable when gold rises
- Believing production automatically scales with price increases
- Overlooking debt and financing structures
- Ignoring geopolitical or operational disruptions

Mining is a capital intensive industry. It requires equipment, labor, energy, compliance, and long term planning. Unexpected costs can disrupt even the most optimistic projections.

Mining stocks are not simply gold proxies. They are complex businesses operating in challenging environments.

Last Thoughts

Understanding what gold and silver mining stocks actually represent is the first step toward rational decision making. These are not pieces of metal. They are shares in corporations that operate within the broader global economy.

Before considering whether they belong in your portfolio, it is important to understand how they function, how they generate revenue, and why their performance depends on more than just metal prices.

In the next chapter, we will take a deeper look at how mining companies actually make money and why profitability is never guaranteed, even in rising metal markets.

Chapter 2: How Mining Companies Actually Make Money

At first glance, the business model of a mining company may appear straightforward. A company extracts gold or silver from the ground and sells it at the prevailing market price. If metal prices rise, profits should rise as well. If prices fall, profits decline.

In practice, the process is far more complex.

Mining is one of the most capital intensive industries in the world. Before a company produces a single ounce of gold or silver, it must invest substantial capital into exploration, land acquisition, geological studies, permitting, infrastructure development, and equipment. The path from discovery to production can take years, sometimes even a decade. Understanding how money flows through this process is critical before viewing mining stocks as simple metal exposure.

Revenue Generation in Mining

Mining companies generate revenue by selling refined gold or silver into global commodity markets. The price they receive is generally tied to the spot price, although some firms use hedging strategies to lock in future selling prices in order to reduce volatility.

Revenue depends primarily on two variables:

- Total ounces produced
- The market price received per ounce

Production levels are influenced by the size of the deposit, the grade of the ore, and the operational capacity of the mine. A large scale producer with multiple operating mines has a very different revenue profile than a small company with a single project.

However, revenue alone tells only part of the story. What ultimately determines success is how efficiently that revenue is converted into profit.

Production Costs and Margins

Mining companies face multiple layers of expense. These typically include:

- Exploration and development spending
- Heavy equipment and machinery
- Energy and fuel
- Labor
- Transportation and refining

- Environmental compliance
- Corporate administration

These costs can fluctuate based on geography, fuel prices, labor markets, and regulatory changes.

Profit margin is the difference between the selling price of the metal and the total cost required to extract and process it. When gold or silver prices rise while costs remain stable, margins expand. But if costs rise due to inflation, labor shortages, or operational inefficiencies, those margins can narrow quickly.

This is why rising metal prices do not automatically guarantee strong earnings. Cost discipline is just as important as price movement.

All In Sustaining Costs Explained

A term you will often encounter when analyzing mining companies is All In Sustaining Costs, commonly referred to as AISC. This metric attempts to capture the full cost of producing an ounce of metal while maintaining ongoing operations.

AISC generally includes:

- Direct mining and processing costs

- Corporate administrative expenses
- Sustaining capital investments
- Equipment maintenance and infrastructure upkeep

Unlike simple operating costs, AISC reflects the reality that mines require continuous reinvestment to sustain production levels.

For example, if gold is trading at $2,000 per ounce and a company reports an AISC of $1,700 per ounce, the apparent margin is $300. But if energy costs increase or additional capital spending becomes necessary, that margin can shrink quickly.

AISC provides a clearer and more realistic view of operational health than revenue figures alone.

The Role of Metal Prices

Gold and silver prices play a central role in mining profitability, but they are influenced by broader macroeconomic forces. Inflation expectations, interest rate changes, currency fluctuations, central bank policies, and geopolitical developments all affect precious metal prices.

Mining companies operate within that pricing environment, yet they have no control over it. They are price takers. Even a well managed mining company can experience earnings pressure if macroeconomic conditions push metal prices lower.

Conversely, strong metal prices can temporarily improve margins, even for companies with operational weaknesses.

Why Profitability Is Not Guaranteed

Mining is inherently uncertain. Geological projections can differ from reality. Ore grades may decline over time. Development projects can exceed budget estimates. Regulatory approvals may be delayed. Political instability in mining regions can disrupt operations entirely.

Many mining companies also rely on financing to fund exploration and development. This can introduce debt risk or lead to the issuance of new shares, which dilutes existing shareholders.

Unlike physical gold, which simply exists as a store of value, mining companies must continually reinvest capital to sustain production. Without ongoing investment, output declines. This capital intensity adds another layer of complexity to the business model.

Last Thoughts

Mining companies generate revenue by extracting and selling precious metals, but their profitability depends on far more than gold or silver prices alone. Operational efficiency, cost management, capital discipline, and macroeconomic conditions all shape financial performance.

Understanding these mechanics helps shift the focus from price speculation to business analysis. Mining stocks represent ownership in corporations that operate within a dynamic and often unpredictable environment.

In the next chapter, we will examine the different categories of mining companies and how their risk profiles vary depending on size, maturity, and stage of development.

Chapter 3: Types of Mining Companies and Their Risk Levels

Not all mining companies operate at the same stage of development. Some are large, established producers with multiple active mines. Others are small exploration firms searching for deposits that may or may not ever become operational.

Understanding the differences between these categories is essential because risk levels vary significantly. A beginner looking at mining stocks without recognizing these distinctions may assume they are all exposed to metal prices in the same way. That assumption can lead to poor decision making.

Major Producers

Major producers are large mining companies with multiple operating mines, diversified geographic exposure, and established production histories. These firms often produce hundreds of thousands, or even millions, of ounces annually.

Because of their scale, major producers tend to have:

- Diversified revenue streams across multiple mines
- Greater access to financing

- More stable production output
- Broader institutional ownership

They are generally considered the least volatile segment of the mining sector. However, that does not mean they are low risk. They still face operational, geopolitical, and commodity price exposure.

Majors may not experience explosive upside during bull markets, but they often demonstrate greater resilience during downturns compared to smaller firms.

Mid Tier Producers

Mid tier producers fall between major corporations and small speculative firms. They typically operate one to several producing mines and may still be expanding.

These companies often offer a blend of:

- Growth potential
- Moderate production stability
- Higher sensitivity to metal prices than majors

Because mid tier firms are still growing, they may reinvest heavily into new projects. This can increase both opportunity and risk. A successful expansion can significantly improve production capacity. A failed project can strain the balance sheet.

Mid tiers often appeal to investors seeking growth without taking on the highest level of exploration risk.

Junior Miners

Junior miners are smaller companies, often focused on developing a single project. Some juniors are early stage producers, while others are still in the development phase.

These companies tend to be:

- More sensitive to financing conditions
- Highly dependent on one primary asset
- More volatile in share price

Juniors can offer significant upside if they successfully move from development to production. However, they also carry higher operational and financing risk. Delays in permitting, cost overruns, or weaker metal prices can severely impact their ability to move forward.

Because juniors often lack diversified revenue streams, setbacks can have outsized consequences.

Exploration Companies

Exploration companies represent the earliest and most speculative stage in the mining lifecycle. These firms are primarily engaged in searching for viable mineral deposits. They may not generate revenue at all.

Their business model typically involves:

- Conducting geological surveys
- Drilling exploratory holes
- Estimating resource potential
- Raising capital through equity issuance

Exploration companies depend almost entirely on investor funding. If they discover a promising deposit, their share price can increase dramatically. If exploration results are disappointing, valuations can decline just as quickly.

These firms represent the highest risk category within the mining sector. Success is uncertain, timelines are long, and profitability may be years away.

Risk Spectrum Comparison

When comparing these categories, it is helpful to think in terms of a spectrum.

- Major producers tend to offer relative stability and scale.
- Mid tier producers balance growth potential with moderate operational exposure.
- Junior miners carry concentrated project risk and higher volatility.
- Exploration companies represent pure speculation on discovery potential.

As you move down this spectrum, potential reward may increase, but so does uncertainty.

Risk tolerance plays a significant role in determining which category, if any, aligns with an investor's objectives. Some investors prefer established companies with diversified operations. Others are willing to accept greater volatility in exchange for the possibility of substantial returns.

The key is understanding what stage of the mining lifecycle you are investing in.

Last Thoughts

Mining companies are not interchangeable. Size, production history, financing structure, and stage of development all influence risk exposure.

Before evaluating financial metrics or projecting future performance, it is important to identify where a company sits within the mining lifecycle. A major producer and an early stage exploration company may both be labeled as gold stocks, but their risk profiles are fundamentally different.

In the next chapter, we will move beyond company size and examine operational risks that affect mining companies regardless of category.

Chapter 4: Operational Risks Most Beginners Overlook

When investors think about mining stocks, they often focus on metal prices. If gold rises, mining stocks should rise. If silver climbs, profits should improve.

But price is only one variable.

Mining is a physical, labor intensive, regulation heavy business. It operates in real world environments with real world constraints. Operational risk can impact production regardless of whether metal prices are rising or falling.

Understanding these risks is essential before evaluating any mining company.

Geopolitical Risk

Mining operations are often located in developing regions where mineral deposits are abundant. While these regions may offer resource potential, they can also introduce political instability.

Geopolitical risk can include:

- Government policy changes
- Increased taxation or royalty rates
- Nationalization of assets
- Civil unrest

- Trade restrictions

A mine located in a politically stable country may carry a different risk profile than one operating in a region with shifting regulatory frameworks.

Investors should pay attention to where a company's assets are located, not just how much metal they produce.

Environmental and Regulatory Risk

Mining is heavily regulated. Governments impose environmental standards, land use restrictions, and permitting requirements that can delay or restrict operations.

Companies must comply with:

- Environmental impact assessments
- Waste management standards
- Water usage regulations
- Land reclamation obligations

Failure to meet regulatory standards can result in fines, operational shutdowns, or loss of permits.

In addition, environmental opposition can delay new projects for years. Even after a deposit is discovered, the path to production is not guaranteed.

Management Execution Risk

Mining projects require strong leadership. Capital allocation decisions, operational planning, and cost management all depend on management quality.

Poor execution can show up in several ways:

- Budget overruns
- Missed production targets
- Inefficient capital spending
- Overly aggressive expansion strategies

Even in a strong gold price environment, weak management can undermine profitability.

Because mining projects often take years to develop, leadership discipline plays a significant role in long term outcomes.

Labor and Supply Chain Disruptions

Mining depends on skilled labor, heavy machinery, energy supply, and transportation infrastructure.

Operational disruptions can arise from:

- Labor strikes
- Skilled labor shortages
- Fuel cost spikes
- Equipment breakdowns

- Transportation bottlenecks

For example, rising fuel costs can materially increase operating expenses. A shortage of skilled workers can delay production timelines. Supply chain disruptions can limit access to replacement parts.

These risks are external to metal prices, yet they directly impact output and margins.

Mine Depletion and Reserve Uncertainty

Mines are not permanent assets. Every deposit has a finite lifespan. Over time, high grade ore may be depleted, leaving lower grade material that is more expensive to process.

Companies must continually invest in exploration to replace depleted reserves.

Reserve uncertainty can arise when:

- Estimated ore grades differ from actual results
- Geological models prove inaccurate
- Production declines faster than projected

If a company fails to replenish reserves, long term production may decline, even if gold or silver prices remain strong.

Mining is not just about current output. It is about sustaining output over time.

Last Thoughts

Operational risk is often overlooked by beginners who focus primarily on gold and silver price movements. But mining companies operate in complex environments shaped by politics, regulation, labor markets, and geological realities.

A strong metal price does not eliminate operational challenges. Production delays, cost overruns, regulatory hurdles, and reserve depletion can all impact profitability.

Understanding these risks shifts the analysis from simple commodity exposure to business evaluation.

In the next chapter, we will examine financial risks and balance sheet analysis, which add another layer of complexity to mining stock evaluation.

Chapter 5: Financial Risks and Balance Sheet Analysis

Operational risk is only one side of the equation. Even if a mining company manages its projects well, financial structure can determine whether it survives downturns or struggles under pressure.

Again, mining is capital intensive. Exploration, development, and expansion require significant funding. Because of this, financial risk plays a central role in the mining sector.

Before investing in any mining stock, it is important to examine how the company finances its operations and how resilient its balance sheet is during weaker metal markets.

Debt and Leverage

Many mining companies use debt to fund exploration and development. Borrowing allows them to build infrastructure and begin production without immediately issuing large amounts of new shares.

However, debt introduces fixed obligations. Interest payments must be made regardless of metal prices.

If gold or silver prices decline, a company with high debt may face pressure. Revenue can fall while debt servicing costs remain constant. In extreme cases, this can lead to asset sales, restructuring, or bankruptcy.

A company with moderate debt and strong cash flow flexibility generally has more room to navigate volatile markets than a highly leveraged firm.

Debt is not inherently negative. The key question is whether it is manageable relative to revenue and cash flow.

Cash Flow Stability

Cash flow tells you how much money a company generates from its core operations after covering operating expenses.

Positive and consistent cash flow allows a mining company to:

- Fund expansion projects internally
- Reduce reliance on external financing
- Weather temporary price downturns

If a company consistently burns cash, it may need to raise capital repeatedly. That can introduce additional risk for shareholders.

Metal prices fluctuate. Companies with stronger cash flow discipline tend to handle those fluctuations more effectively than those relying heavily on optimistic price assumptions.

Dilution Through Share Issuance

When mining companies need capital, one common method is issuing new shares. This raises money without increasing debt, but it reduces the ownership percentage of existing shareholders.

This process is known as dilution.

Dilution becomes more common among junior and exploration companies that do not yet generate meaningful revenue. Each new capital raise can expand the total share count, meaning existing shareholders own a smaller portion of the company.

Even if a project eventually succeeds, repeated dilution can limit upside per share.

Understanding share count trends over time is important. A growing production profile combined with stable share count can signal financial discipline. Rapidly increasing share count may signal heavy dependence on equity financing.

Capital Expenditure Requirements

Mining projects require ongoing capital expenditure, often referred to as CAPEX. This includes building new infrastructure, upgrading equipment, and developing additional resource zones.

CAPEX is typically divided into two categories:

- Initial capital expenditures used to build or acquire a project

- Sustaining capital expenditures used to maintain existing operations

High capital requirements can delay profitability. A company may report promising production estimates, but if large capital investments are required upfront, investors must evaluate how those projects will be financed.

If financing depends on optimistic future metal prices, risk increases.

Reading Basic Financial Statements

Even beginners can review a few core financial indicators without needing advanced accounting knowledge.

When reviewing financial statements, consider:

- Revenue growth trends
- Operating margins
- Total debt relative to cash
- Free cash flow
- Share count changes over time

You do not need to become a financial analyst, but understanding these fundamentals helps separate narrative from numbers.

Mining companies often present optimistic production forecasts. Financial statements show whether those projections are translating into sustainable performance.

Last Thoughts

Financial risk can amplify both opportunity and downside in mining stocks. Debt levels, cash flow stability, capital expenditure demands, and share dilution all shape long term outcomes.

A company may operate a promising deposit, but if its balance sheet is weak, volatility in metal prices can create significant strain.

Evaluating mining stocks requires looking beyond production headlines and focusing on financial durability. In the next chapter, we will explore why mining stocks do not always track gold and silver prices as closely as many investors assume.

Chapter 6: Why Mining Stocks Do Not Always Track Gold and Silver Prices

One of the most common assumptions beginners make is that mining stocks move in direct proportion to gold or silver prices. If gold rises 10 percent, mining stocks should rise 10 percent or more. If silver declines, mining stocks should fall.

In reality, the relationship is far more complex.

Mining stocks are equities. They trade within the broader stock market. Their performance reflects not only metal prices, but also investor sentiment, liquidity conditions, and overall market trends.

Understanding this disconnect is critical before treating mining stocks as simple proxies for precious metals.

Market Sentiment vs Metal Prices

Stock prices are influenced by expectations. Investors do not simply react to current metal prices. They react to what they believe will happen next.

If gold prices are rising but investors expect a reversal, mining stocks may underperform. Conversely, mining stocks may rally before gold prices rise if investors anticipate future gains.

This forward looking nature of equity markets creates periods where mining stocks and metal prices diverge.

Sentiment can sometimes outweigh fundamentals in the short term.

Equity Market Correlation

Mining stocks are part of the broader equity ecosystem. During strong stock market rallies, capital often flows into growth sectors such as technology or consumer discretionary companies. In such environments, mining stocks may lag even if metal prices are stable.

During broad market downturns, investors may sell equities across the board to raise liquidity. In these moments, mining stocks can decline alongside the broader market, even if gold prices are rising.

This phenomenon highlights an important distinction:

Gold is a commodity. Mining stocks are equities.

Equities are influenced by overall risk appetite in financial markets.

Liquidity and Volatility

Liquidity conditions also play a role. When financial markets tighten and capital becomes scarce, smaller mining companies can experience amplified volatility.

Junior miners in particular may see exaggerated price swings because:

- They have lower trading volume
- They rely more heavily on investor capital
- They are more sensitive to shifts in risk tolerance

Even if gold remains stable, reduced market liquidity can pressure share prices.

Volatility does not always reflect changes in operational performance. Sometimes it reflects changes in capital flows.

Speculative Cycles

Mining stocks often move in cycles. During precious metal bull markets, enthusiasm can build quickly. Investors may project continued price appreciation and bid up shares aggressively.

In these phases, valuations may expand beyond what current earnings justify.

When sentiment shifts, those same stocks can decline rapidly, even if gold or silver prices remain elevated.

These cycles can create the illusion that mining stocks are unreliable proxies for metal prices. In truth, they are reacting not just to current prices, but to changing expectations about future profitability.

Case Style Example of Divergence

Consider a scenario where gold rises from $1,800 to $2,000 per ounce over several months. On the surface, this should improve mining company margins.

However, during that same period:

- Energy costs may increase
- Equity markets may decline
- Investors may reduce exposure to risk assets
- Financing conditions may tighten

Under these conditions, mining stocks could remain flat or even decline, despite rising gold prices.

The stock market does not isolate one variable. It evaluates the entire operating environment.

Last Thoughts

Mining stocks are influenced by gold and silver prices, but they are not governed by them alone. Equity market conditions, liquidity, investor expectations, and macroeconomic trends all shape performance.

This is why treating mining stocks as simple metal substitutes can lead to misunderstanding.

Recognizing the difference between commodity price exposure and equity market exposure helps build a more realistic framework for evaluating mining stocks.

In the next chapter, we will explore behavioral economics and how investor psychology plays a role in mining stock speculation.

Chapter 7: Behavioral Economics and Speculation

Mining stocks do not move based on numbers alone. They move based on human behavior.

While financial statements, production reports, and metal prices provide data, investor psychology often determines how that data is interpreted. During strong bull markets, optimism can expand far beyond fundamentals. During downturns, fear can overshadow long term potential.

Understanding behavioral economics helps explain why mining stocks can become highly speculative, even when underlying business conditions have not changed dramatically.

Herd Behavior in Bull Markets

When gold or silver begins rising sharply, attention follows. Financial media coverage increases. Online discussions multiply. Investors observe others entering the sector and feel pressure to participate.

This is known as herd behavior.

As more capital flows into mining stocks, prices can rise quickly. The momentum itself becomes part of the attraction. Rising prices reinforce the belief that further gains are inevitable.

In these environments, valuations may expand faster than underlying earnings. Investors are not only buying current performance. They are buying expectation.

Herd behavior can sustain rallies longer than fundamentals alone would justify.

Fear of Missing Out

> Closely related to herd behavior is the fear of missing out, often referred to as FOMO. When mining stocks rise rapidly, investors may feel they are falling behind if they do not participate.

This urgency can lead to decisions based more on recent price movement than careful analysis.

Instead of evaluating:

- Production costs
- Balance sheet strength
- Reserve sustainability

Investors may focus primarily on short term price acceleration.

FOMO does not necessarily reflect poor intelligence. It reflects emotional response to momentum. Recognizing it can help prevent impulsive entry points.

Media Amplification and Narrative Cycles

Financial narratives often follow cycles. When precious metals begin rising, stories about inflation, currency weakness, and safe haven demand become more prominent.

Mining companies may be portrayed as high growth beneficiaries of these trends. Positive narratives can attract additional speculative capital, which pushes prices higher, reinforcing the narrative.

Eventually, expectations can become detached from operational reality.

When narratives shift, the reversal can be equally rapid. Media coverage turns cautious. Analysts revise projections downward. Investors who entered based on excitement may exit based on fear.

Narrative cycles amplify volatility.

Loss Aversion and Panic Selling

Behavioral research shows that people experience losses more intensely than gains. In mining stocks, this dynamic can create sharp downside moves.

When prices decline, some investors hold positions hoping for a recovery. Others exit quickly to avoid further losses. As selling pressure builds, prices can fall faster than fundamentals would suggest.

Loss aversion can cause investors to sell near market lows, just as fear of missing out can cause them to buy near market highs.

Both reactions are driven by emotion rather than structured evaluation.

Overconfidence and Confirmation Bias

In bull markets, investors may become overly confident in their analysis. Positive price movement reinforces the belief that their thesis is correct.

Confirmation bias can then emerge. Investors seek information that supports their optimism and disregard data that challenges it.

For example, rising gold prices may overshadow:

- Rising production costs
- Increasing debt
- Reserve depletion

- Political instability in operating regions

When sentiment is strong, warning signs can be overlooked.

Recognizing these tendencies does not eliminate them, but it creates awareness.

Last Thoughts

Mining stocks operate at the intersection of commodity markets and equity markets. That intersection amplifies behavioral dynamics.

Excitement during metal rallies and fear during downturns can push prices beyond what operational fundamentals alone would justify.

Understanding behavioral economics does not guarantee better returns, but it can promote discipline. Recognizing herd behavior, fear of missing out, loss aversion, and overconfidence helps shift decision making from emotional reaction to structured analysis.

In the next chapter, we will return to fundamentals and examine mining stocks as businesses first, and metal plays second.

Chapter 8: Mining Stocks as Businesses First, Metal Plays Second

It is easy to think of mining stocks as extensions of gold or silver. When metal prices rise, interest in mining shares increases. When metal prices fall, enthusiasm fades.

But at their core, mining stocks are businesses.

They generate revenue, manage expenses, allocate capital, hire executives, issue shares, and answer to shareholders. Viewing them primarily as metal proxies can obscure the fact that they operate within the same corporate framework as any other publicly traded company.

Understanding mining companies as businesses first, and metal plays second, creates a more grounded perspective.

Corporate Governance

Corporate governance refers to how a company is structured, managed, and overseen. This includes the board of directors, executive leadership, and internal decision making processes.

Strong governance can improve:

- Capital allocation discipline

- Risk management practices
- Transparency with shareholders
- Long term strategic planning

Weak governance can result in excessive executive compensation, poorly timed acquisitions, or risky expansion projects.

Because mining projects often involve large capital expenditures and long timelines, leadership quality plays a significant role in long term outcomes.

Executive Incentives

Executives are typically compensated through a mix of salary, bonuses, and stock based incentives. The structure of those incentives can influence decision making.

For example, short term performance bonuses tied to share price may encourage aggressive expansion or optimistic projections. Long term incentive structures tied to sustainable production and cash flow may encourage more disciplined growth.

Investors who review compensation disclosures can gain insight into how management priorities align with shareholder interests.

Incentives shape behavior. In capital intensive industries like mining, incentive alignment matters.

Shareholder Priorities

Mining companies answer to shareholders. Some investors prioritize dividend payments. Others prioritize production growth or exploration expansion.

Large institutional investors may influence strategic direction, especially in major producers. Junior companies may rely heavily on retail investors seeking growth potential.

Balancing these expectations can be challenging. A company that prioritizes aggressive growth may reinvest heavily rather than return capital to shareholders. A company focused on stability may limit expansion.

Understanding a company's stated strategy helps clarify what type of investor it is attempting to attract.

Mergers and Acquisitions

The mining industry frequently experiences mergers and acquisitions. Larger companies may acquire smaller firms to expand reserves or enter new geographic regions.

Acquisitions can create value if assets are integrated efficiently and purchased at reasonable valuations.

However, they can also introduce integration challenges, unexpected costs, or excessive debt.

When metal prices are high, acquisition activity often increases. Companies may compete aggressively for promising deposits. Timing matters. Paying high valuations during peak cycles can reduce long term returns.

Evaluating acquisition strategy is another way to assess whether management prioritizes disciplined growth.

Long Term Sustainability

A mining company's long term success depends on its ability to replace depleted reserves and manage environmental responsibilities.

Sustainability includes:

- Ongoing exploration to replenish resources
- Responsible environmental practices
- Community engagement in operating regions
- Financial resilience across commodity cycles

Mining is not static. Deposits are finite. Without reinvestment and strategic planning, production eventually declines.

Companies that balance profitability with long term reserve development often demonstrate greater durability across cycles.

Last Thoughts

Mining stocks represent ownership in operating businesses, not simply exposure to metal prices. Governance quality, executive incentives, capital allocation decisions, and acquisition strategy all influence outcomes.

When evaluating mining stocks, it is helpful to step back from daily price fluctuations and consider the broader corporate structure. A rising gold price may improve margins temporarily, but sustainable performance depends on disciplined management and strategic execution.

In the next chapter, we will directly compare mining stocks with physical metals to highlight the structural differences between corporate ownership and tangible asset ownership.

Chapter 9: Mining Stocks vs Physical Metals

At this point, we have examined mining companies as businesses. Now it is helpful to step back and compare mining stocks directly with physical gold and silver.

Both provide exposure to precious metals, but they function very differently. Understanding those structural differences allows investors to determine which approach, if any, aligns with their objectives.

The comparison is not about declaring one superior to the other. It is about recognizing how each behaves within a portfolio.

Control and Custody

When you own physical gold or silver, you control a tangible asset. You can store it at home, in a vault, or with a custodian. Its value fluctuates with the market price of the metal, but ownership itself does not depend on corporate performance.

When you own a mining stock, you own shares in a company. Your exposure depends on management execution, operational efficiency, financing decisions, and broader equity market conditions.

Physical metal does not require quarterly earnings reports. Mining companies do.

This difference in structure creates different types of risk.

Counterparty Risk

Physical gold and silver generally carry minimal counterparty risk when held directly. The value depends on the global market for the metal, not on the solvency of a corporation.

Mining stocks introduce corporate risk. Shareholders depend on:

- Management integrity
- Financial stability
- Operational success
- Regulatory compliance

If a mining company encounters financial distress, shareholders may face losses independent of metal prices.

This does not make mining stocks inherently negative, but it does make them structurally different from physical holdings.

Insurance vs Speculation

Physical gold and silver are often described as wealth preservation assets. They tend to attract investors seeking stability during periods of uncertainty.

Mining stocks, on the other hand, may appeal to investors seeking growth. Because of operating leverage, they can amplify movements in metal prices. That amplification can create opportunity, but it also increases volatility.

In practical terms, physical metals often serve as a form of financial insurance. Mining stocks function more like growth oriented equity investments tied to commodity cycles.

The distinction lies in purpose.

Volatility Comparison

Mining stocks typically exhibit greater price volatility than physical metals.

This is due to several factors:

- Exposure to broader equity market swings
- Sensitivity to earnings expectations

- Financing conditions
- Speculative capital flows

Physical metals fluctuate as well, but they are not influenced by corporate earnings reports or shareholder sentiment.

For investors sensitive to large price swings, this difference can matter significantly.

Portfolio Role Differences

The role each asset plays in a portfolio may vary depending on investor objectives.

Physical metals may be included for diversification, inflation hedging, or long term preservation. Mining stocks may be included for potential capital appreciation tied to commodity cycles.

Some investors choose to hold both, allocating different portions of capital based on risk tolerance.

The important factor is clarity of intention. Without clarity, it is easy to treat mining stocks as substitutes for physical metal when they operate under entirely different dynamics.

Last Thoughts

Mining stocks and physical metals both relate to gold and silver, but they do not behave the same way. One represents ownership in a corporation. The other represents direct ownership of a tangible asset.

Understanding this structural difference helps prevent unrealistic expectations. A mining stock is not simply a bar of gold in digital form. It carries business risk, equity market exposure, and management execution risk.

In the next chapter, we will bring everything together and build a rational framework for evaluating whether mining stocks belong in your overall investment strategy.

Chapter 10: Building a Rational Framework Before Investing

By now, you understand that gold and silver mining stocks are not simple metal substitutes. They are operating businesses influenced by commodity prices, operational execution, financial structure, and investor psychology.

The question is no longer whether mining stocks can rise. The more important question is whether they align with your objectives, risk tolerance, and strategy.

Before investing, it helps to create a rational framework. A framework does not eliminate risk, but it encourages structured decision making rather than reactive behavior.

Defining Your Investment Objective

Every investment should serve a purpose.

Are you seeking:

- Long term capital appreciation
- Short term trading opportunities
- Portfolio diversification

- Exposure to precious metal cycles

Mining stocks may fit some of these objectives better than others.

If your primary goal is wealth preservation, your analysis may differ from someone seeking aggressive growth. Clarity at the outset reduces the likelihood of misalignment later.

Risk Tolerance Assessment

Mining stocks can experience significant volatility. Price swings may occur due to earnings reports, metal price fluctuations, geopolitical developments, or changes in investor sentiment.

Ask yourself:

- How do you respond to short term losses?
- Are you comfortable with large price fluctuations?
- Would a 20 percent decline alter your long term conviction?

Risk tolerance is not about optimism. It is about emotional and financial resilience.

Understanding your tolerance level helps prevent decisions driven by panic or overconfidence.

Position Sizing Principles

Even when an investment thesis appears strong, concentration increases risk. Position sizing determines how much of your portfolio is allocated to a specific asset.

A measured approach may involve:

- Limiting mining stocks to a defined percentage of total portfolio value
- Diversifying across company size categories
- Avoiding overexposure to a single project or region

Position sizing cannot eliminate volatility, but it can contain its impact.

Diversification Considerations

Mining stocks represent a specific segment of the commodity and equity markets. Diversification across asset classes can reduce overall portfolio risk.

Diversification may include balancing mining stocks with:

- Physical metals
- Broader equity exposure
- Fixed income assets
- Cash reserves

The goal is not to eliminate risk, but to avoid dependence on a single outcome. Commodity cycles can last years. A diversified structure helps navigate those cycles with greater stability.

When Walking Away Is the Smartest Decision

Education before speculation means recognizing when an investment does not align with your strategy.

After evaluating operational risk, financial structure, behavioral influences, and personal objectives, you may conclude that mining stocks are not appropriate for your portfolio.

That conclusion is not a failure. It reflects disciplined analysis. Investing is not about participating in every opportunity. It is about selecting opportunities that fit within a structured plan.

Last Thoughts

Building a rational framework requires stepping back from excitement and focusing on fundamentals. Mining stocks can offer opportunity, but they also carry layered risks that extend beyond metal prices.

By defining objectives, assessing risk tolerance, sizing positions carefully, and diversifying appropriately, investors can approach the sector with greater clarity.

Education does not guarantee success. It does, however, improve decision quality.

In the final section, we will summarize the core principles discussed throughout this book and reinforce the central theme: education before speculation.

Conclusion: Education Before Speculation

Gold and silver mining stocks attract attention for understandable reasons. They offer exposure to precious metals, potential operating leverage, and the possibility of capital appreciation during strong commodity cycles.

But throughout this book, one theme has remained consistent: mining stocks are not simple extensions of metal prices. They are operating businesses influenced by geology, regulation, management decisions, financing conditions, equity market sentiment, and investor psychology.

Understanding that distinction changes the way you evaluate them.

We examined how mining companies generate revenue and how production costs shape profitability. We explored the differences between major producers, mid tier companies, junior miners, and exploration firms. We discussed operational risks, financial structure, dilution, and capital requirements. We also examined why mining stocks do not always move in direct proportion to gold or silver prices.

Most importantly, we addressed the behavioral side of investing. Speculation often intensifies during metal rallies. Expectations expand. Narratives strengthen. Price momentum attracts additional capital. Without a structured framework, it becomes easy to confuse enthusiasm with analysis.

Education before speculation means slowing down that process.

It means asking:

- What stage of development is this company in?
- How strong is its balance sheet?
- How exposed is it to operational and geopolitical risk?
- How much of my portfolio am I allocating?
- Does this investment align with my broader objectives?

These questions do not eliminate uncertainty. Mining will always involve risk. Commodity markets will always fluctuate. Investor sentiment will continue to shift between optimism and caution.

But disciplined evaluation creates clarity.

You may decide that mining stocks fit a portion of your portfolio. You may decide that direct metal ownership better suits your goals. Or you may decide that neither aligns with your current strategy.

The outcome matters less than the process.

When decisions are based on structured analysis rather than excitement, long term results tend to reflect greater consistency. Markets will continue to move. Cycles will continue to repeat. Education provides the foundation for navigating those cycles without being carried away by them.

That is the purpose of this book.

Education before speculation.

www.ingramcontent.com/pod-product-compliance
Lightning Source LLC
LaVergne TN
LVHW022317200926
848481LV00004B/1368